T0197591

CHRIST WILL RETURN! ARE YOU READY?

WILL YOUR NAME APPEAR IN THE LAMB'S BOOK OF LIFE?

**Minister
Jeanette McDonald**

WestBow Press books may be ordered through booksellers or by contacting:

WestBow Press
A Division of Thomas Nelson & Zondervan
1663 Liberty Drive
Bloomington, IN 47403
www.westbowpress.com
844-714-3454

Scripture taken from the King James Version of the Bible.
Heaven (The Holy City), Copyright © 1990 by Jeanette McDonald. All rights reserved.
Are We Sitting On A Time Bomb? Copyright © 1990 by Jeanette McDonald. All rights reserved.
Hope, Copyright © 1990 by Jeanette McDonald. All rights reserved.
Heaven's Bank, Copyright © 1990 by Jeanette McDonald. All rights reserved.

ISBN: 978-1-4497-4015-3 (sc)
ISBN: 978-1-4497-5411-2 (e)

Library of Congress Control Number: 2012902643

Print information available on the last page.

WestBow Press rev. date: 10/07/2021

WestBow
PRESS®
A DIVISION OF THOMAS NELSON
& ZONDERVAN

Get ready, be ready,

Stay ready, the hour

When Christ shall

Return is not recorded.

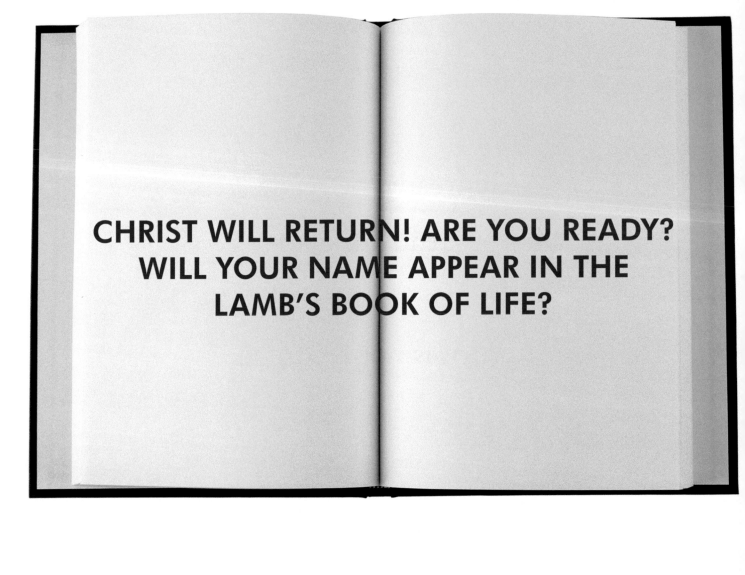

<u>Dedication</u>

In loving memory of my grandmother Zacle Haliburton, my sister Debbie Jackson, and my parents Maurice and Vera Davis, I thank God for being the daughter of my mentors.

To my loving husband Larry McDonald Sr., my son Robert Mack Jr. and my granddaughter Kaitlyn Mack.

To my sisters Linda Timmons, Lorraine Davis-Quick, Clarice Davis, Maurice Manning, Dionne Ford and my brothers Edwin Davis, Billy Davis, Pastor Michael D. Davis for all their love and support.

A special thank you to Elder Dock Timmons Jr.

To all readers of this book, thank you for supporting me. I pray that you experience a life change.

May God Bless and Keep all of you,

Jeanette McDonald

Heaven's Bank

Heaven's bank has plenty space
Invest your interest it is a holy place

Heaven's bank has a miraculous saving plan
For pious people living on this land

Heaven's bank has credit to last
Provided your sins stay in the past

Heaven's bank greatest loan to us
Jesus giving his life with no fuss

Heaven's bank is overstocked with everlasting love
From the Father and son sitting graciously above

Heaven's bank consist of praising God's name
With a spotless life free of sin and shame

Heaven's bank is the best place to go
Weeping and gnashing will happen below

__Hope__

The rain will cease to pour upon you
The Sun dries up the rain and dew

Sunshine and gladness will come soon
To help diminish your dark afternoon

There are moments one gives up hope
Over painful situations too hard to cope

During hard times or moments of sorrow
Visualize your thoughts of a pleasant tomorrow

Are We Sitting On A Time Bomb?

Our destinations are uncertain on this earth
The creator has known before our birth

Problems are numerous all over these lands
We can do nothing, they are out of our hands

People are murdered and thrown into some weeds
No one on earth can stop these horrible deeds

It is impossible to know what tomorrow might hold
We are always hearing grievous stories told

They are saying the air is full of pollution
Will any scientists find a solution?

People are frightened of what to expect
Dreary things are happening too hard to detect

When we lie down and close our eyes at night
We could be awakened in a terrible freight

From hearing a sudden bursting eruption
Or will it be the world's destruction?

Heaven (The Holy City)

Heaven is the holy city with streets paved of gold
All can enter there in, young and old

Heaven is the holy city, where saints will go
All unrighteous and ungodly will appear below

God will wipe away all your tears
Suffering will be yesterday, from past years

Living eternally with Jesus makes you glad
Nothing in Heaven will make you sad

Saints will rejoice praising God forever
Thanking him for gathering them together

Heaven and The Lake of Fire are two locations people will spend eternity. Heaven is the throne of God, a dwelling place for deity angels and souls of the redeemed. Heaven is a holy city with streets paved of gold, with precious gemstones around the city. All born again people (who eschewed evil and suffered for Christ sake) will enter into this holy city and live with Christ for eternity. A rapture will occur. During the rapture, Jesus shall send his angels to gather his elect from earth to heaven. God's elect will rejoice praising the name of the Lord for eternity. There is no sickness, no sorrow, no dying, no crying, no pain in heaven your past life will be changed.

The Lake of Fire burning with brimstone is where the ungodly people will be cast into a bottomless pit for eternity. There will be weeping and gnashing of the teeth. Matthew 8:12 The ungodly people will fall and continue to fall in this bottomless pit for eternity. The ungodly people shall be burned as in an oven. Malachi 4:1

For, behold, the day cometh, that shall burn as an oven; and all the proud, yea, and all that do wickedly, shall be stubble: and the day that cometh shall bun them up, saith the LORD of hosts, that it shall leave them neither root nor branch. Malachi 4:1

God gave me a personal experience about the Lake of Fire. I fell in a dark bottomless pit, my arms and legs fell off from the elements of the heat. I was falling head first; a strong force was pulling me down in that bottomless pit. It was so dark; I could not see anyone or anything.

It was so dark, I could not see anyone or anything. I continued to fall down in that pit and heard voices coming from people I could not see.

The people were full of anxiety yelling, "We want to get out of here." I was full of anxiety myself, yelling along with the other voices coming from that bottomless pit stating, "I wanted to get out of that place." People were so tormented in that place. I heard some voices coming from a lower area in that bottomless pit stating, "It's too late, and you cannot get out of here!" The Lord allowed me to go down low enough in that pit to see the flames. God allowed my head to get close to the flames and then the Lord got me out of that dark bottomless pit. I believe, God gave me an outer body experience to warn others.

"AND I SAW ANOTHER ANGEL FLY IN THE MIDST OF HEAVEN, HAVING THE EVERLASTING GOSPEL TO PREACH UNTO THEM THAT DWELL ON THE EARTH, AND TO EVERY NATION, AND KINDRED, AND TONGUE, AND PEOPLE, SAYING WITH A LOUD VOICE, FEAR GOD, AND GIVE GLORY TO HIM; FOR THE HOUR OF HIS JUDGMENT IS COME: AND WORSHIP HIM THAT MADE HEAVEN, AND EARTH, AND THE SEA, AND THE FOUNTAINS OF WATERS."

REVELATION XIV. 6, 7.

The Lord gave me another experience, about a large oven door. The oven door was large enough to fit my entire body. I was standing in front of this large oven door full of flames. Someone pushed me in and shut the door. I was sitting in the oven full of flames and smelt my flesh cooking. I felt as though I was suffocating. The Lord allowed me to remain in there a short period of time to visualize the lake of fire is actual. I believe in my heart this was an outer body experience. God is awesome and powerful. He can do anything. Nothing is impossible with God. When my experience was over; the large oven door popped open. I was released and came out. I believe God gave me two supernatural experiences, so I could warn others against the lake of fire.

In a vision, God showed me two people covered in flames. They were in agony and screaming from the torment. I could not tell the gender of those in torment.

Hell exists and people will be cast into it. Hell enlarged its' mouth for an apparent reason. No one should want to spend eternity burning and being tormented in the Lake of Fire.

Jesus redeemed the whole world, when he shed his precious blood on Calvary's cross. We can be saved through Christ Jesus and not face eternal damnation. J e s u s made it possible for us to escape; the Wrath of God. We must repent, ask him to forgive us for our sins and be born again to live a life free from sin and shame. Once we repent, God remembers no more our ungodly deeds. We are new creatures in Christ having a second chance in life to live Godly choosing good over evil.

I admonish you to repent for your sins of commission. Ask God to forgive your sins while there is still time and blood runs warm in your veins. You must confess with your mouth and believe in your heart, God raised Jesus from the dead and thou shalt be saved. Romans 10:9

That if thou shalt confess with thy mouth the Lord Jesus, and shalt believe in thine heart that God hath raised him from the dead, thou shalt be saved. Romans 10:9

Jesus said, "Behold I stand at the door, and knock: if any man hear my voice, and open the door, I will come in to him and will sup with him, and he with me." Revelation 3:20

After you repent for your sins of commission de- velop a new relationship with the Lord through prayer. Read the Bible daily to prevent Satan from tempting you to revert to your old life. When you read the bible you will learn obedience and allegiance pleases God.

God wants you to fast. Fasting means to do without food for a period of time. As we fast, God wants you to meditate and get a closer walk with him. It cleanses you spiritually and naturally. Jesus fasted forty days and forty nights. Matthew 4:2

And when he had fasted forty days and forty nights, he was afterward an hungered. Matthew 4:2

Study to show thyself approved unto God, a workman that needeth not to be ashamed, rightly dividing the word of truth. II Timothy 2:15

The gospell of S. Mathew.
The fyrst Chapter.

Thys ys the boke of the generaciõ of Jesus Christ the soñe of David/The sonne also of Abra cħã.

Abraham begatt Isaac:

Isaac begatt Jacob:

Jacob begatt Judas and hys bre= (thren:

Judas begat Phares:
and Zaram of thamar:

Phares begatt Esrom:

Esrom begatt Aram:

Aram begatt Aminadab:

Aminadab begatt naassan:

Naasson begatt Salmon:

Salmon begatt boos of rahab:

Boos begatt obed of ruth:

Obed begatt Jesse:

Jesse begatt david the kynge:

David the kynge begatt Solomon/of her that was the (wyfe of vry:

Solomon begat roboam:

Roboam begatt Abia:

Abia begatt asa:

Asa begatt iosaphat:

Josaphat begatt Joram:

Joram begatt Osias:

Osias begatt Joatham:

Joatham begatt Achas:

Achas begatt Ezechias:

Ezechias begatt Manasses:

Manasses begatt Amon:

Amon begatt Josias:

Josias begatt Jechonias and his brethren about the tyme of the captivite of babilen

After they were led captive to babilen/ Jechonias begatt

Reverence the two great commandments: Thou shalt love the Lord thy God with all thy heart, soul, and mind. This is the first and great commandment. The second is like unto it. Thou shalt love thy neighbor as thyself. Matthew 22:37-39

Jesus said unto him, Thou shalt love the Lord thy God with all heart, and with all thy soul, and with all thy mind. This is the first and great commandment. And the second is like unto it, Thou shalt love thy neighbor as thyself. Matthew 22:37-39

Jesus said for us to love our enemies do good to those who despitefully use and persecute you. Matthew 5:44-46 for if you love them who love you, what reward has ye?

But I say unto you, Love your enemies, bless them that curse you, do good to them that hate you, and pray for them which despitefully use you, and persecute you;

That ye may be the children of your Father which is in heaven: for he maketh his sun to rise on the evil and on the good, and sendth rain on the just and on the unjust.

For if ye love them which love you, what reward have ye? do not even the publicans the same? Matthew 5:44-46

Jesus said, "To let your light shine before men that they may see your good works and glorify the Father in heaven." Matthew 5:16

Let your light so shine before men, that they may see your good works, and glorify your Father which is in heaven. Matthew 5:16

God spared not the angels that sinned, but cast them into chains of darkness to be reserved unto judgment. II Peter 2:4 And Noah the eighth person, a preacher of righteousness bringing in the flood upon the world of the ungodly. II Peter 2:5 And turning the cities of Sodom and Gomorrah into ashes condemned them with an over- throw making them an example, unto those that after should live ungodly. II Peter 2:6 God will not excuse ungodly behavior.

And spared not the old world, but saved Noah the eighth person, a preacher righteousness, bringing in the flood upon the world of the ungodly; II Peter 2:5

But the fearful and unbelieving and the abominable, and murders, and whoremongers, and sorcerers, and idolaters, and all liars, shall have their part in the lake which burneth with fire and brimstone: which the second death.

Revelation 21:8

The heavens shall pass away with a great noise and the elements shall melt with fervent heat and the earth also, and the works that are therein shall be burned up. II Peter 3:10 Jesus will separate wheat from the tares. Only, what we do for Christ will last.

And he shall send his angels with a great sound of a trumpet, and they shall gather together his elect from the four winds, from one end of heaven to the other. Matthew 24:31

Some of the recordings of John the Divine from the book of Revelation:

John said: And I saw the dead small and great stand before God: and the books were opened, and another book was opened, which is the book of life: and the dead were judged out of those things which were written in the books according to their works. Revelation 20:12 and the sea gave up the dead who were in it: and death and hell delivered up the dead who were in them and they were judged every man according to their works. Revelation 20:13 and death and hell were cast into the lake of fire, this is the second death. Revelation 20:14 and whosoever was not found written in the book of life was cast into the lake of fire. Revelation 20:15

The End Times

In the last days perilous times shall come. Men shall be lovers of themselves covetous, boasters, proud, blasphemers disobedient to parents, unthankful, unholy. Without natural affection trucebreakers, false accusers, in continent fierce despisers of those that are good. Traitors' heady high-minded lovers of pleasure more than lovers by God. Having a form of godliness but denying the power thereof from such turn away. II Timothy 3:1-5

This knows also, that in the last days perilous times shall come. For men shall be lovers of their own selves, covetous, boasters, proud, blasphemers, disobedient to parents, unthankful, unholy, Without natural affection, trucebreakers, false accusers, incontinent, fierce, despisers of those that are good, Traitors, heady, high-minded, lovers of pleasures more than lovers of God; Having a form of godliness, but denying the power thereof: from such turn away. II Timothy 3:1-5

Brethren ye know yourselves the times and seasons, that the day of the Lord cometh as a thief in the night. For when they say peace and safety then sudden destruction cometh upon them as is travail upon a woman with child and they shall not escape. I Thessalonians 5:3

For when they shall say, Peace and safety; then sudden destruction cometh upon them, as travail upon a woman with a child; and they shall not escape. I Thessalonians 5:3

But ye, brethren are not in darkness, that that day should overtake you as a thief. I Thessalonians 5:4

Mothers are against daughters, and daughters are against mothers, fathers are against sons, and sons are against fathers. Brothers are betraying each other to death. Children will rise up and murder their parents, parents are murdering their children. People are murdering their entire families and killing themselves. People are so perplexed. They are doing so many ungodly horrific things. If these perplexed people would surrender their lives to Jesus, he would give them a new mind, a new heart, a new talk, and a new walk. Therefore, these people would become a new creature in Christ Jesus.

The End Times

For as lightening cometh out of the east and shineth even unto the west so shall also the coming of the Son of man be. Matthew 24:27 I admonish you do not revert to your old life, remain saved. Jesus told Nicodemus, "Verily, verily, I say unto thee Except a man be born of the water and of the spirit he can not enter into the kingdom of God." John 3:3 Jesus was talking to Nicodemus in this verse, but everyone must be born again, if they want to enter God's kingdom. Blessed are they that do his commandments that they may have right to the tree of life, and may enter in through the gates of the city. Revelation 22:14 Jesus said: behold I come quickly: hold that fast which thou hast, that no man take thy crown. Revelation 3:11 Jesus said: behold I come quickly blessed is he that watcheth and keep his garment lest he walk naked and they see his shame. Revelation 16:15 Jesus said: behold I come quickly; and my reward is with me, to give every man according as his works shall be. Revelation 22:12

And, behold I come quickly; and my reward is with me, to give every man according as his work shall be. Revelation 22:12

There shall be signs and wonders in the sun, and in the moon, and in the stars and upon the earth in distress of nations, with perplexing; the sea roaring. Luke 21:25

And there shall be signs in the sun, and in the moon, and in the stars; and upon the earth distress of nations, with perplexity; the sea and the wave roaring; Luke 21:25

Men's hearts failing them for fear, looking after those things coming on the earth for the power of heaven shall be shaken. Luke 21:26

Men's heart failing them for fear, and for looking after those things which are coming on the earth: for the powers of heaven shall be shaken. Luke 21:26

Many people shall come in Christ's name, saying they are the Christ and shall deceive many, you shall hear of wars and rumors of wars. Be not troubled for these things must come to pass, but the end is not yet.

Nations shall rise against nation, kingdom against kingdom, there shall be famines (famine is starvation), pestilences (pestilences are different kinds of diseases). There shall be earthquakes in divers places. All these are the beginning of sorrow.

False prophets shall rise up and deceive many, because iniquity shall abound,the love of many shall wax cold.

Jesus said unto them, Thou shalt love the Lord thy God with all thy heart,and with the soul, and with all thy mind. This is the first and great commandment. And the second is like unto it, Thou shalt love thy neighbor as thyself. Matthew22:37-39

As in the days of Noe were, so shall also the coming of the Son of man be. Matthew 24 : 37

For in the days before the flood they were eating and drinking marrying and giving in marriage, until the day that Noe entered into the Ark. Matthew 24:38. And knew not until the flood came and took them all away, so shall also the coming of the Son of man be. Matthew 24:39 Watch therefore: ye know not what hour your Lord doth come. Matthew 24: 42; But know this, that if the goodman of the house known in what watch the thief would come he would have watched, and would not have suffered his house to be broken up. Matthew 24: 43 Therefore be ye also ready: for in such an hour as ye think not the Son of man cometh. Matthew 24:44 Blessed is that servant, whom his Lord when he cometh shall find so doing. Matthew 24:46 Jesus was speaking in parables about the natural side so we would understand the spiritual side.

(Read Matthew Chapter 24)

Get ready, be ready, stay ready, the hour when Christ shall return is not given to man. The time is not recorded, but God in heaven alone, knows the day when Christ will appear. Christ will return ready or not. Make sure you're washed in the blood of the lamb, Jesus cleansing blood. Keep you garments spotless and be prayerful and watchful until Christ comes.

If you are ready to live with Christ for eternity, when he comes, your name should appear in the lamb's book of life.

God bless you and God keep you.

Time is like a silent clock (tick tock tick tock). Time is winding down on us. I was inspired by our Lord and Savior Jesus Christ to write this book.

Author Biography

Minister Jeanette McDonald has genuine love and compassion for people. She has a fire to preach God's word. She is an intercessor and prophetess. She received a Missionary license on July 28, 1996. Minister McDonald was ordained and licensed on January 27, 2008. She has written a book of inspirational poems and a book for children. Writings of Jeanette McDonald were published for a VA hospital and Whataburger employee newsletter. Minister McDonald is a gospel soloist. She has written and recorded songs. Creative art, cooking, and writing are her passions. Truly, Minister Jeanette McDonald has an awesome testimony of personal devastation and how God restored more to her life than what the enemy stole. She knows, God rewards those who diligently seek him. Aside from writing, Minister Jeanette McDonald is a loving wife, mother of one son, grandmother of one granddaughter. She is currently serving at House of Prayer The Beauty of Holiness Church, Pastor Michael D. Davis, Sr. and his wife Brenda Davis.

Printed in the United States
by Baker & Taylor Publisher Services